Head Louse

Karen Hartley,
Chris Macro,
and Philip Taylor

Heinemann Library
Chicago, Illinois

Designed by Ron Kamen
Illustrated by Alan Fraser at Pennant Illustration
Originated by Ambassador Litho
Printed in China by South China Printing Co. Ltd.
04 03 02 01
10 9 8 7 6 5 4 3 2

Library of Congress Cataloging-in-Publication Data
Hartley, Karen, 1949-
    Head louse / Karen Hartley, Chris Macro, Philip Taylor.
        p. cm. – (Bug books)
    Includes bibliographical references (p.) and index.
    Summary: An introduction to head lice, discussing how they are born, what they look like, what they eat, how they grow, where they live, and how to get rid of them.
    ISBN 1-57572-549-5 (lib. bdg.)
    1. Pediculosis—Juvenile literature. 2. Lice—Juvenile literature. [1. Pediculosis. 2. Lice.] I. Macro, Chris, 1940- II. Taylor, Philip, 1949- III. Title. IV. Series.
RL764.P4 H37 2000
616.5'7—dc21   99-057442

Acknowledgments

The Publishers would like to thank the following for permission to reproduce photographs:

NHPA/G.I. Bernard, p. 4; Science Gallery, p. 5; NHPA/Stephen Dalton, pp. 6, 25; Science Photo Library/Andrew Syred, p. 7; Science Photo Library/Dr. P. Marazzi, p. 8; Ardea London/John Mason, p. 9; Science Photo Library/Dr. Chris Hale, p. 10; London Scientific Films, p. 11; Scott Camazine, p. 12; Oxford Scientific Films/J.A.L. Cooke, pp. 13, 21, 22; Premaphotos Wildlife/Ken Preston-Mafham, p. 14; Oxford Scientific Films/Alastair MacEwen, p. 15; Science Photo Library/M. Clarke, p. 16; Bubbles/Ian West, p. 17; Tony Stone/Charles Thatcher, p. 18; Tony Stone/Caroline Wood, p. 19; Science Photo Library/Bsip Vem, p. 20; Nature Photographers/Nicholas Phelps Brown, p. 23; Bubbles/Jennie Woodcock, pp. 24, 27; Science Photo Library/Eye of Science, p. 26; Bubbles/James Lamb, p. 28; Sinclair Stammers, p. 29.

Cover photograph reproduced with permission of JAL Cooke/Oxford Scientific Films.
Every effort has been made to contact copyright holders of any material reproduced in this book. Any omissions will be rectified in subsequent printings if notice is given to the Publisher.

Some words are shown in bold, **like this.** You can find out what they mean by looking in the glossary.

Contents

What Are Head Lice?

Head lice are **insects**. They live in people's hair. When they move around and feed, they make your head feel itchy.

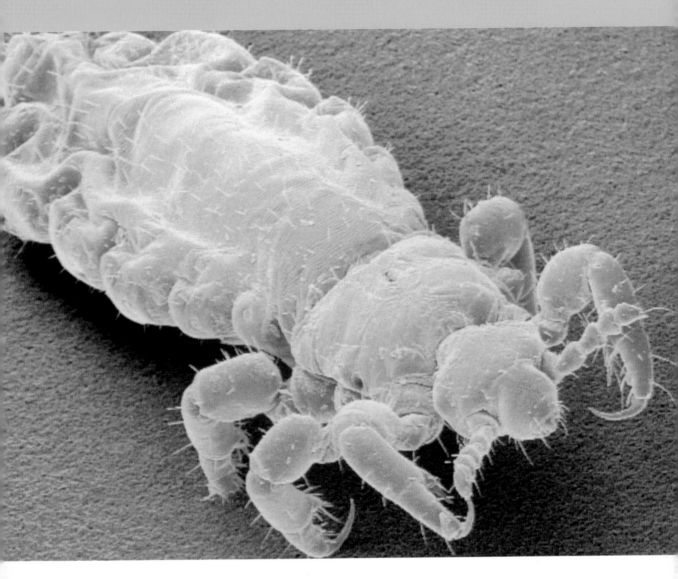

All lice are **parasites**. Different types
live on other animals, in their fur or
hair. Some suck and others chew. The
human head louse is a sucking louse.

What Head Lice Look Like

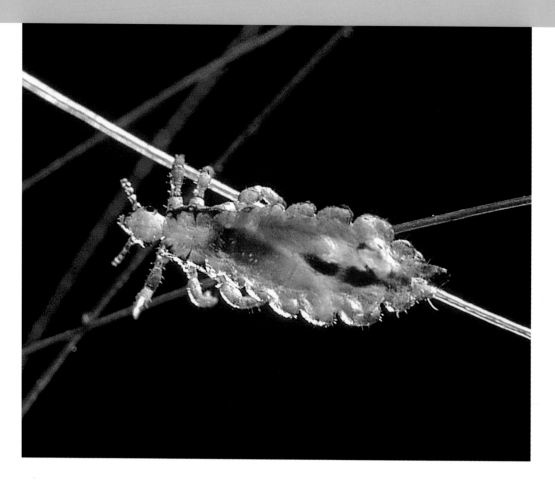

Head lice do not have wings. They have short **antennae**. Their bodies are soft and flat. Sometimes head lice are white, and sometimes they are brown.

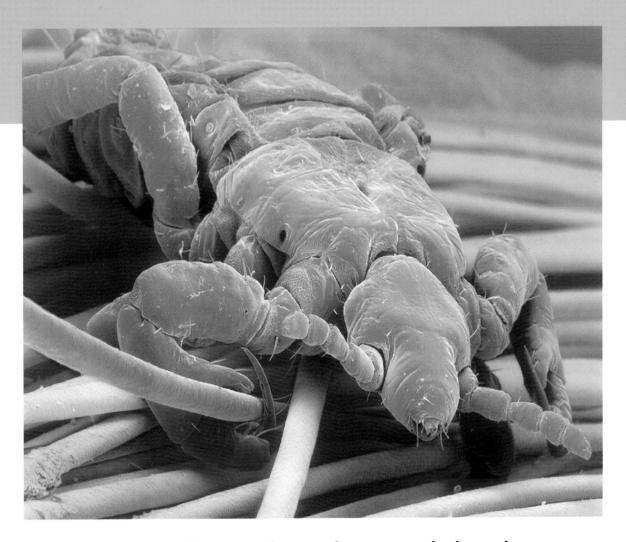

Head lice have short legs with hooks, which help them to hold onto hairs on our heads. They have sharp mouthparts called **stylets** that they stick into people's heads.

How Big Are Head Lice?

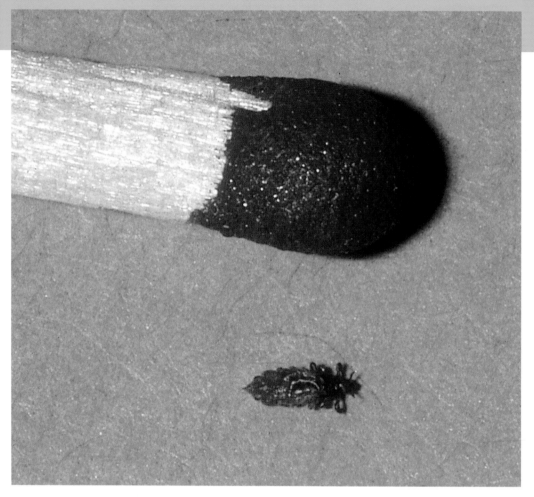

Head lice are hard to see because they are very tiny. They are about as big as the head of a pin. Female head lice are bigger than male head lice.

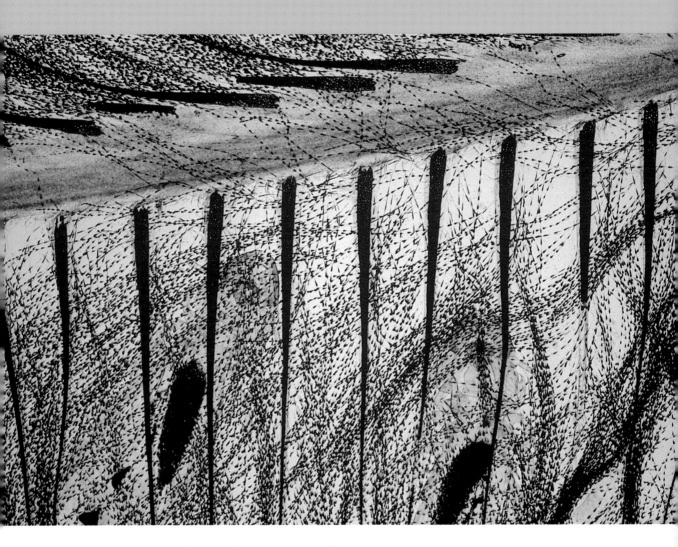

Some other kinds of lice have bigger heads and smaller bodies than human head lice. Chewing lice live on birds and eat bits of skin and feathers. They do not suck blood for food.

How Head Lice Are Born

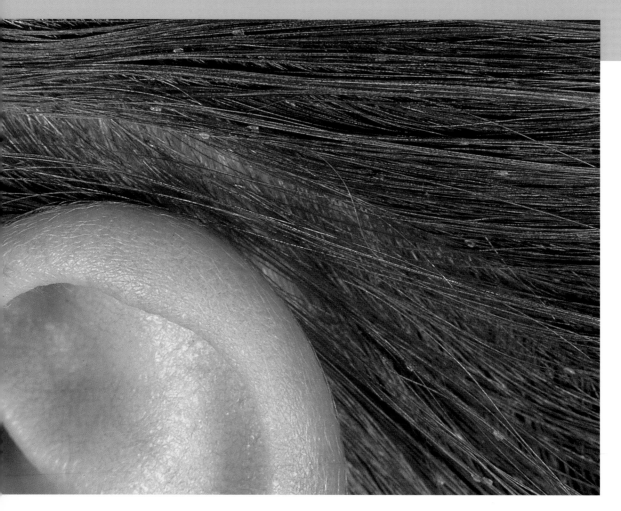

Adult head lice lay about six eggs a day. They make a glue to stick each egg, or **nit**, to a hair. The eggs can be laid one by one or in groups.

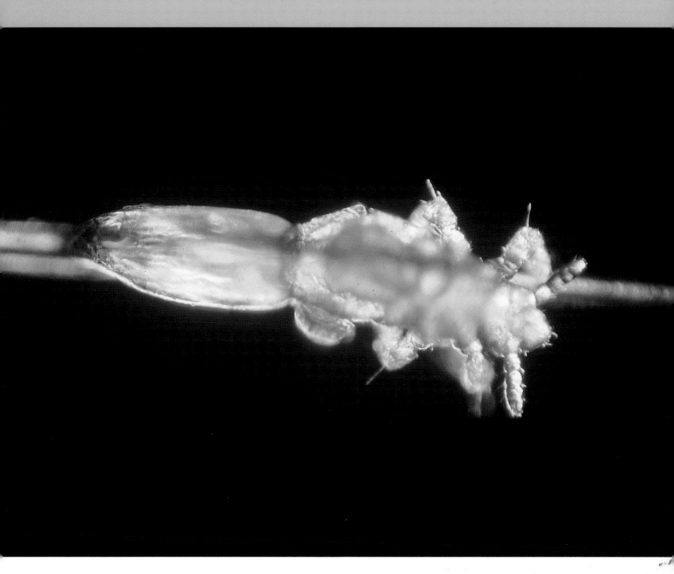

When the baby inside the egg is ready to **hatch**, it sucks in air. Blowing the air out helps to push it from the egg. The empty eggshells are also called nits.

How Head Lice Grow

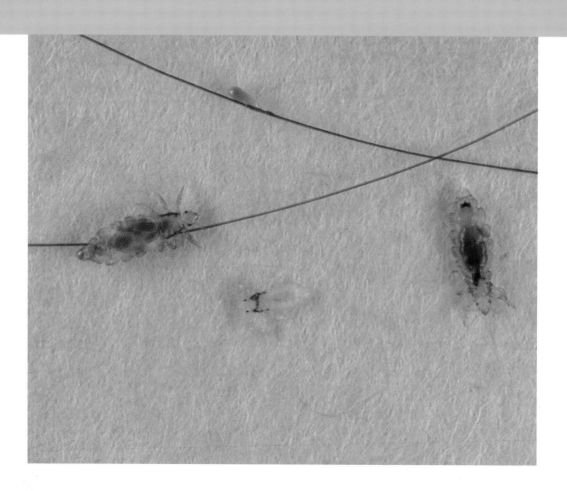

Baby head lice are called **nymphs**. The nymphs are **transparent**. As they grow, they change color to match the color of the hair they live on.

When the nymph grows too big for its skin, the skin falls off. This is called **molting**. There is a new, bigger skin underneath. After a nymph has molted three times, it is an **adult**.

What Head Lice Eat

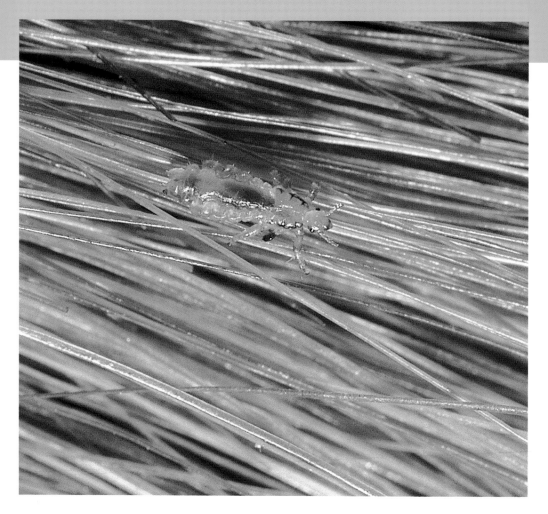

Human head lice eat only blood, which they suck from their **host's** head. They need to feed several times a day in order to get enough to eat.

When the head lice are ready to eat,
they make a hole in the skin with their
stylets. Then they suck the blood
through these special tubes.

How We Attack Head Lice

People feel dirty if they have lice in their hair. Anyone can catch them, and many people do. An **adult** can comb your hair and look for the tiny white **nits**.

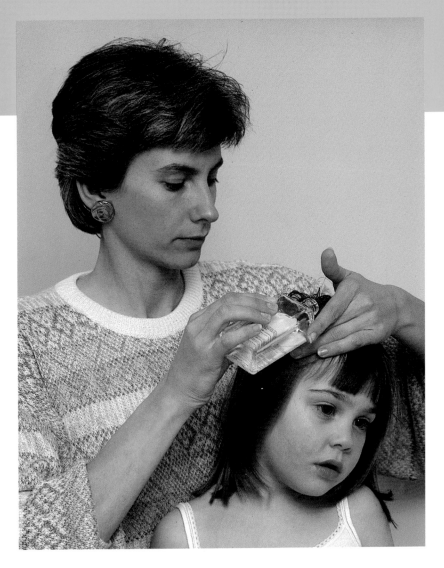

The only way to get rid of lice is to kill them. An adult can wash your hair with a special cream. The chemicals in the cream kill the lice, so no more eggs can be laid.

Where Head Lice Live

A head louse will usually spend its whole life on the head of the same person. Head lice can live in the hair of people from all countries. Head lice can live on **adults** as well as on children.

If head lice leave their **host** for too long, they will die. They need our blood and the warmth of our heads to live.

How Head Lice Move

Head lice have three pairs of legs on the front parts of their bodies. Lice cannot jump, but they can crawl along the hair when people's heads touch each other. This is one way they can be passed on.

Head lice can also crawl onto your head when you share hats, coats, hairbrushes, combs, and other things that someone with lice has used.

How Long Head Lice Live

The whole life of a head louse is only about a month long. In this time, a louse can grow big and **mate**. A female louse can lay all her eggs.

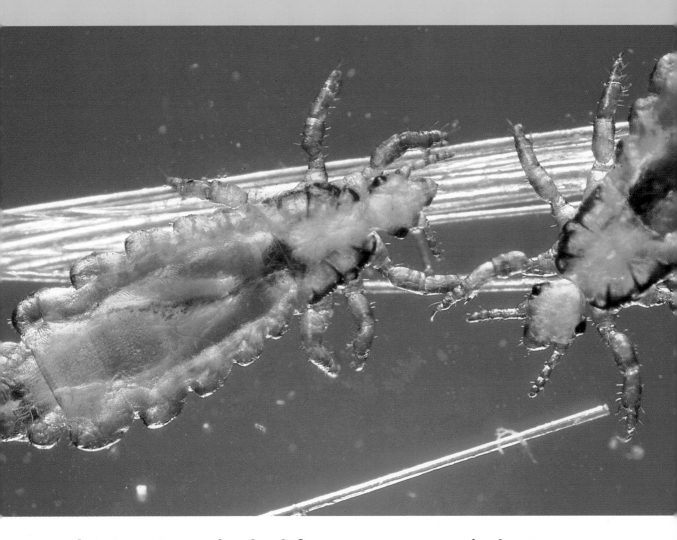

Living its whole life in someone's hair means that a head louse stays at about the same **temperature**. If the head louse becomes much hotter or colder, it will die even sooner.

What Head Lice Do

When another person's head is very close, head lice can feel the heat of the person's body. The lice may crawl onto the other person's head, or they may stay where they are.

Some people think that only people with dirty hair have head lice. This is not true. Head lice can cling easily to both clean and dirty hair.

How Are Head Lice Special?

Although head lice have two eyes, one on each side of the head, they cannot see very well. They can only tell when it is light or dark.

Head lice squirt a special liquid into our heads so that we cannot feel them sucking our blood. This liquid makes the **wounds** itch afterwards.

Thinking about Head Lice

Think about what you know about head lice. Can you think why people should wash their hair often and never share hats or combs?

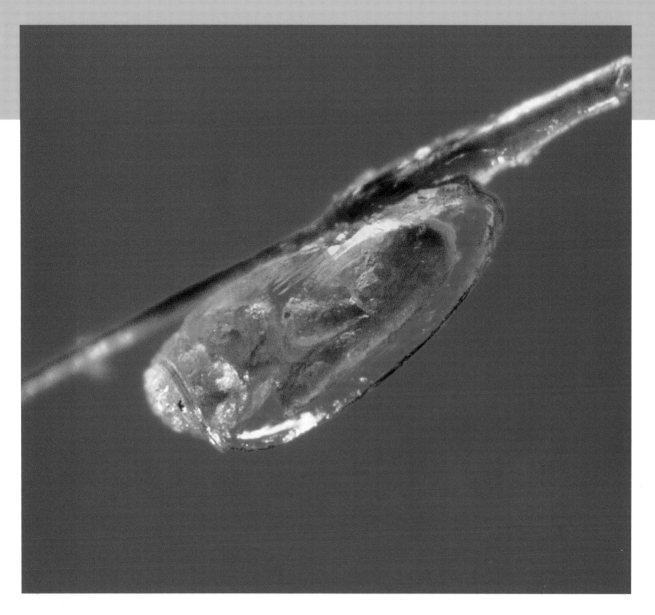

Think about the picture on this page.
Do you know if it is a picture of an egg,
a **nymph**, or an **adult** head louse?

Bug Map

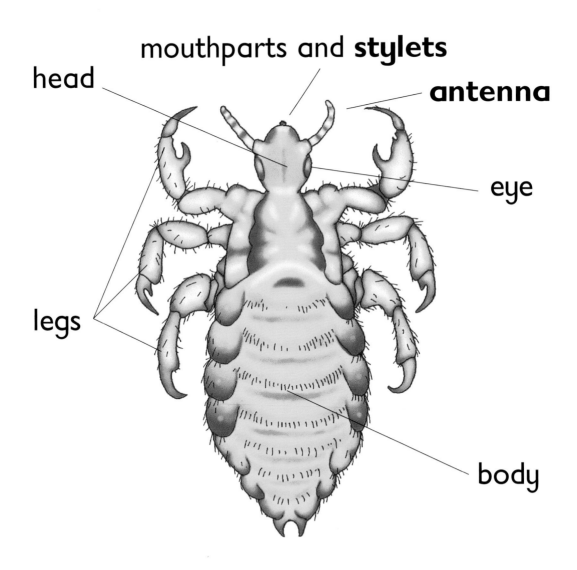

head

mouthparts and **stylets**

antenna

eye

legs

body

Glossary

adult grown-up

antenna (more than one are antennae) thin tube on an insect's head that may be used to smell, feel, or hear

hatch to come out of an egg

host person or animal on which a louse lives

insect small animal with six legs

mate when a male and a female come together to make babies

molt to shed an old skin that is too small

nit egg or empty eggshell

nymph baby head louse

parasite animal that lives on another animal

stylet thin, sharp tube used for making a hole in the skin and sucking blood

temperature how hot or cold something is

transparent able to be seen through

wound sore place on the body

More Books to Read

Caffey, Donna. *Yikes—Lice!* Morton Grove, Ill.: Albert Whitman & Company, 1998.

Gordon, Melanie A. *Let's Talk about Head Lice.* New York: The Rosen Publishing Group, Inc., 1999.

Merrick, Patrick. *Lice.* Chanhassen, Minn.: The Child's World, Inc., 1999.

Index